The Prayers of S

W. H. Griffith Thomas

Alpha Editions

This edition published in 2024

ISBN 9789361474507

Design and Setting By

Alpha Editions
www.alphaedis.com

Email - info@alphaedis.com

As per information held with us this book is in Public Domain.
This book is a reproduction of an important historical work.
Alpha Editions uses the best technology to reproduce historical work
in the same manner it was first published to preserve its original nature.
Any marks or number seen are left intentionally to preserve.

Contents

GENERAL PREFACE	- 1 -
I.	- 2 -
II.	- 6 -
III.	- 10 -
IV.	- 14 -
V.	- 20 -
VI.	- 26 -
VII.	- 32 -
VIII.	- 39 -
IX.	- 44 -
APPENDIX.	- 49 -

GENERAL PREFACE

The title of the present series is a sufficient indication of its purpose. Few preachers, or congregations, will face the long courses of expository lectures which characterised the preaching of the past, but there is a growing conviction on the part of some that an occasional short course, of six or eight connected studies on one definite theme, is a necessity of their mental and ministerial life. It is at this point the projected series would strike in. It would suggest to those who are mapping out a scheme of work for the future a variety of subjects which might possibly be utilised in this way.

The appeal, however, will not be restricted to ministers or preachers. The various volumes will meet the needs of laymen and Sabbath-school teachers who are interested in a scholarly but also practical exposition of Bible history and doctrine. In the hands of office-bearers and mission-workers the "Short Course Series" may easily become one of the most convenient and valuable of Bible helps.

It need scarcely be added that while an effort has been made to secure, as far as possible, a general uniformity in the scope and character of the series, the final responsibility for the special interpretations and opinions introduced into the separate volumes, rests entirely with the individual contributors.

A detailed list of the authors and their subjects will be found at the close of each volume.

I.

GRACE AND HOLINESS.

"Now God Himself and our Father, and our Lord Jesus Christ, direct our way unto you. And the Lord make you to increase and abound in love one toward another, and toward all men, even as we do toward you: To the end He may stablish your hearts unblameable in holiness before God, even our Father, at the coming of our Lord Jesus Christ with all His saints."—1 THESS. iii. 11-13.

There are few more precious subjects for meditation and imitation than the prayers and intercessions of the great Apostle. He was a man of action because he was first and foremost a man of prayer. To him both aspects of the well-known motto were true: "To pray is to labour," and "To labour is to pray."

There is no argument for or justification of prayer; nor even an explanation. It is assumed to be the natural and inevitable expression of spiritual life. Most of the Apostle's prayers of which we have a record are concerned with other people rather than with himself, and they thus reveal to us indirectly but very really what St. Paul felt to be the predominant needs of the spiritual life.

In this series of studies we propose to look at some of these prayers, and to consider their direct bearing upon our own lives. Taking the Epistles in what is generally regarded to be their chronological order, we naturally commence with the prayer found in 1 Thess. iii. 11-13. In this passage we have what is not often found, a prayer for himself associated with prayer for others.

1. HIS PRAYER FOR HIMSELF (ver. 11).

Let us notice *Who it is to Whom he prays*—"God Himself and our Father, and our Lord Jesus Christ." The association of Christ with God as One to Whom prayer is addressed is of course very familiar to us, but it ought never to be forgotten that when the Apostle penned these words the association was both striking and significant. For consider: these words were written within twenty-five years of our Lord's earthly life and ascension, and yet here is this quiet but clear association of Him with the Father, thus testifying in a very remarkable and convincing way to His Godhead as the Hearer of prayer. And this fact is still more noticeable in the original, for St. Paul in this verse breaks one of the familiar rules of grammar, whether of Greek or English. It is well known that whenever there are two nouns to a verb the verb must be in the plural; and yet here the Greek word "direct" is in the singular, notwithstanding the fact that there are two subjects, the Father and Christ. The same feature is to be found in 2 Thess. ii. 17. It is evident from this what St. Paul thought of our Lord Jesus Christ, and it is in such simple, indirect testimonies that we find the strongest and most convincing proofs that the early Church believed in the Deity of our Lord.

Let us consider *what it is for which he prays*—"Direct our way." He asks for guidance. There had been certain difficulties in the way of his return to Thessalonica. He had been hindered, and now asks that God would open the way for him to go back to his beloved friends. Nothing was outside the Apostle's relationship to God, and nothing was too small about which to pray to God. As it has been well said: "Nothing is so small that we do not honour God by asking His guidance of it, or insult Him by taking it out of His hands." The need of guidance is a very real one in every Christian life, and the certainty of guidance is just as real. "The steps of a good man are ordered by the Lord" (Ps. xxxvii. 23); and this is as true now as ever. "I will guide thee with Mine eye" (Ps. xxxii. 8) is a promise for all time, and we may confidently seek guidance in prayer whenever it is needed. The answer to our prayer will come in a threefold way. God guides us by His Spirit, reigning supreme within our hearts. He also guides us by the counsels and principles of His Word. These two agree in one, for the Holy Spirit never guides contrary to the Word. And then, in the third place, He guides us by His Providence, so that when the Word, the Spirit, and Providence in daily circumstances agree we may be sure that the guidance has been given.

2. HIS PRAYER FOR OTHERS (vers. 12, 13).

Consider the *immediate request* he makes—"The Lord make you to increase and abound in love one toward another, and toward all men." He asks for *love* on their behalf, that God would grant them this greatest of all gifts— "the very bond of peace and of all virtues, without which whosoever liveth is counted dead before Him." Love in the New Testament is no mere sentiment, for it involves self-sacrifice. It is not limited to emotion; it expresses itself in energy. It does not evaporate in feeling; it expresses itself in fact. "Love is of God," for "God is love"; and the Apostle in praying this prayer asks for the supreme gift of their lives.

The measure of the gift is noticeable—"Increase and abound in love." The "increase" has to do with their inner life, their hearts being more and more enlarged in capacity to possess this love; the "abounding" has to do with their outward life, and points to the overflow of that love towards others.

Consider, too, the *objects* of this love—"Toward one another, and toward all men." There was, first of all, the special love to be shown toward

Christians, according to the "new commandment" (John xiii. 34). In the New Testament the emphasis is laid again and again upon brother-love, or love of the brethren, and the brotherhood. This was something entirely new in the world's history—a new tie or bond, the union of hearts in Christ Jesus. To see how these Christians loved one another was a proof of this new affection based upon the new commandment. But, further, their love was to extend beyond their fellow-Christians—even to "all men," just as we have in St. Peter's Epistle, in that long chain of graces, first, love of the brethren, and then, love towards all (2 Pet. i. 7).

And yet it may perhaps be asked, How is it possible for us to love everybody? What about those who are not lovely and lovable—how can we love these? It may help us to remember that there is a clear distinction between *loving* and *liking*. While it is impossible to *like* everybody, it is assuredly possible to love everybody. A mother loves her wayward son, but she cannot like him, for there is practically nothing "alike" between them. In the same way we may love with the love of compassion if we cannot love with the love of complacency, and thus fulfil our Lord's command and realise the answer to the Apostle's prayers. This, we may be perfectly certain, is the supreme thing, and our Christianity will count for nothing in the eyes of men if it is not permeated and energised through and through with active, whole-hearted, Christ-like love.

Consider the *ultimate purpose* he expresses—"To the end He may stablish your hearts unblameable in holiness." The love for which he prays is to be expressed in holiness. The meaning of holiness throughout the Old and New Testaments is "separateness." The idea is that of a life separated unto God, dedicated, consecrated to His service. Wherever the words "holiness," "sanctification," and their associated and cognate expressions are found, the root idea is always that of separation rather than of purification. It involves the whole-hearted and entire dedication of the life to God. The cognate word "saint" does not strictly mean "one who is pure," but "one who belongs to God."

The sphere of this holiness is to be in "your hearts." It is always to be noticed that in Scripture the "heart" includes the intellect, the emotions, and the will. In a word, it is the centre of our moral and spiritual being; and when this is understood we can see at once the point and importance of the heart being holy, for it is only another way of saying that our entire being is to be separated from all else in order to be possessed by, and consecrated to, God.

The standard of holiness is also brought before us in this prayer—"Stablish your hearts unblameable in holiness." The Apostle prays that they may be steadfast, not weak and vacillating. The great need was for solidity and steadfastness, as it is in the present day, for it is only when the heart is established by grace and in holiness that it can in any true sense serve God. This emphasis on a fixed or stablished heart is brought before us several times in Holy Scripture (cf. Ps. lvii. 7, cviii. 1, cxii. 7; Heb. xiii. 9).

And steadfast hearts will be "unblameable" hearts, hearts that are not blameworthy. A clear distinction is to be drawn between unblameable hearts and unblemished hearts. A little child may perform a task which in the result is full of blemishes, though the child, having done his best, is entirely without blame. In like manner, though the believer is not free from blemish, it is nevertheless possible for him to live free from blame. This is the meaning of the Apostle, and the reason of his prayer.

In all this we can see the close connection between love and holiness. When our hearts are filled to overflowing with the love of God to us, and of our love to Him, the inevitable result is holiness, a heart separated unto God, "strengthened with all might," and "ready unto every good work."

Consider the *great incentive* he urges—"Before God, even our Father, at the coming of our Lord Jesus Christ with all His saints." The Apostle puts before his readers the great future to which they were to look, and he urges upon them this love and this holiness in the light of the coming of our Lord Jesus Christ, and all that it will mean to the people of God. St. Paul draws a wonderful picture of that day in a very few words. He speaks first of all of God's presence there: "Before God, even our Father." Then he reminds us of the presence of the Lord Jesus Christ. And last of all he tells us that "the saints" will be there also. Thus, surrounded by our fellow-Christians, and in the presence of our God and Saviour, we shall see as we are seen, and know as we are known, with hearts "unblameable in holiness."

This, then, is what the Apostle prays for his beloved friends in Thessalonica—abounding love and perfect holiness. This is Christianity and the normal Christian life. How simple it all is, summed up in the words Love and Holiness. And yet how searching it is! The simplest things are often the most difficult, and while it is possible for the believer to do great things and to shine in great crises, it is not always so easy to go on loving day by day, and to continue growing in grace and holiness, until the heart becomes so stablished in grace that our Christianity becomes the permanent character of our life. Yet this is God's purpose for each one of us. And the fact that the Apostle prayed for this is a clear proof that an answer was expected, and that the purpose can be realised.

II.

CONSECRATION AND PRESERVATION.

"And the very God of peace sanctify you wholly: and I pray God your whole spirit and soul and body be preserved blameless unto the coming of our Lord Jesus Christ. Faithful is He that calleth you, Who also will do it."—1 THESS. v. 23, 24.

As we consider these prayers of the Apostle, we become increasingly aware of what he felt to be the most important elements in the Christian life. The prayers all have reference to Christian living, and whether we think of the character of the life portrayed, or the standard held up in them, we can readily see their intense practical value for daily living. We may be pretty sure that those things for which he prayed on behalf of his converts were the things he regarded as most essential in Christian character and conduct.

The prayer that now calls for consideration is that found in 1 Thess. v. 23, 24.

1. THE PETITION.

He prays for their *sanctification*—"Sanctify you wholly." As already noted, the root idea of sanctification, and of its cognate expressions, "holiness," "holy," and the like, is *separation*. We see this very clearly in connection with buildings or things which are said to be "holy" or "sanctified." It is obvious that no thought of purification is applicable to buildings and inanimate objects. We must, therefore, understand sanctification in this case as equivalent to consecration. This is also the root-meaning of the word "sanctify" in relation to persons, and it may be questioned whether the word, as used in the original, ever really includes in it the idea of purification; the latter thought has another set of words altogether. The Apostle therefore prays that they may be consecrated, set apart from all else, for the possession and service of God. This meaning may be aptly illustrated from our Lord's words about Himself: "For their sakes I *consecrate* Myself, that they also may be *consecrated* through the truth" (John xvii. 19).

The *extent* of this consecration is very noteworthy—"Sanctify you wholly." The word rendered "wholly" is used in connection with the Old Testament sacrifices in the Septuagint, and implies the entire and complete separation of the offering for the purpose intended. The Christian life must be wholly, entirely, and unreservedly consecrated to God, no part being reserved or held back, but everything handed over and regarded as permanently and completely belonging to Him.

He prays for their *preservation*—"Preserved blameless." The consecration is to be maintained in continual preservation, in and for God. The consecration as an act is to be deepened into an attitude, so that, day by day, and hour by hour, the separated life may be maintained, and preserved in readiness for every call that God may make.

The *extent* of this preservation is also observable—"Your whole spirit and soul and body." The spirit is that inmost part of our life which is related to God. The soul is the inner life regarded in itself, as the seat and sphere of intellect, heart, and will. The body is the outward vehicle and expression of the soul and spirit through which we are enabled to serve God. The order of these three should be observed. It is not, as we often say, and sing in certain hymns, "body, soul, and spirit," but the very reverse—"spirit, soul, and body." The Apostle starts from within and works outward, thereby reminding us that if the spirit or deepest part of our nature is wholly surrendered to God, this fact will express itself in every part of our nature, and we shall be consecrated wholly. What a searching requirement this is, and what a solemnity and responsibility it gives to life! Whether in relation to God, or in relation to man, whether for worship or work, character or conduct, prayer or practice, we are to be wholly consecrated, and continually kept for the Master's use—

> "That all my powers with all
> their might,
> In Thy sole glory may unite."

2. THE PRE-REQUISITE.

"The God of Peace Himself." The Divine title associated with this prayer as its definite presupposition and pre-requisite is very significant, as, indeed, is every title of God. There is always some special point of direct connection between the way in which God is addressed and the prayer that follows. In the present instance the prayer for consecration and preservation is addressed to "The God of Peace Himself."

The Apostle lays special stress upon the fact that it is God "Himself" Who consecrates and keeps us. As with salvation, so with consecration—it is and must be Divine. The work is entirely beyond any mere human power, and while there is a truth in our frequent reference to consecration as something that we ourselves have to effect, it is far more scriptural, and, therefore, much more helpful, to endeavour to limit the idea of consecration to the Divine side, and to think of it as an act of God, to which the corresponding human act and attitude is that of *dedication*. It is God Himself Who separates us, marks us off as His own, and designates us for His use and service. It is God Himself, and no one else, for we are here brought into personal and blessed association with the Divine power and grace.

Further, God is described as "The God of Peace," and we naturally ask what it means, and why peace is thus associated with consecration and preservation. This title, "The God of Peace," is found very frequently in the writings of St. Paul, and it deserves careful consideration in each passage. There is a twofold peace in Scripture, sometimes described as "peace with God" (Rom. v. 1), at others as "the peace of God" (Phil. iv. 7); and they both have their source in the "God of Peace" (Phil. iv. 9). Peace is the result of reconciliation with God. Our Lord made peace by the Blood of His Cross (Col. i. 20), and the acceptance of His atoning sacrifice through faith brings peace to the soul. This consciousness of reconciliation in turn causes a blessed sense of restfulness and peace to spring up in the heart, and thus we have the peace of God within us.

The connection between peace and holiness is close and essential. It is impossible for anyone to understand consecration until they have experienced reconciliation. Holiness must be based on righteousness, and righteousness is only possible to those who have accepted the Lord Jesus as God's righteousness through faith. So long as there is any enmity in the heart, or even any uncertainty as to our acceptance in Christ Jesus, holiness is an impossibility. May not the forgetfulness of this fact be the cause of surprise and disappointment at Christian Conventions from time to time? May it not be that many go to such gatherings longing to be made holy who have not settled this question of their standing before God and their peace as the result of acceptance of Christ's atonement? To understand and experience what holiness means before enjoying peace with God is like trying to take a second step before attempting the first. Only through peace can holiness come, and only as we have blessed personal experience of God as the God of peace can a prayer like this be answered.

3. THE PROSPECT.

"Unto the coming of our Lord Jesus Christ." Once again the Apostle prays with special reference to that glorious day to which he was always looking and pointing his readers. As he looks forward to that day he uses again a favourite word, "blameless," and suggests to us the great and wonderful possibility of being so consecrated and preserved that we may lead a blameless life day by day until the coming of our Lord. Holiness is thus associated once again with the great future. The Apostle finds in the coming of the Lord one of the most potent reasons why Christians should be consecrated and preserved. This close and intimate connection between holiness, and what we term the Second Advent, needs much stronger emphasis in daily living and in church teaching than it often has in the present day. There is, in its way, nothing more powerful as a reason for holiness than the thought of the certainty and imminence of the Lord's coming.

4. The Promise.

"Faithful is He that calleth you, Who also will do it." Lest we should be tempted to think that so wonderful a prayer could not be fulfilled in daily experience, the Apostle adds this blessed assurance that God, Who puts this ideal before us, will enable us to realise it. The promise is undoubted—"Who also will do it." What He has promised He is also able to perform. If only our hearts are right with Him, and are willing to say, "Yea, let Him take all," God will, indeed, consecrate and preserve us blameless unto the end. The guarantee of this lies in His Divine faithfulness. "Faithful is He that calleth you." We are touching the bed-rock of Divine revelation when we contemplate the faithfulness of God. This phrase is often found in the New Testament: "God is faithful." "The Lord is faithful." "Faithful is He." "This is a faithful saying." If our hearts will only rest upon this we shall find in it, not only the most exquisite joy and assured peace, but also the ground of our perfect confidence that He will accomplish His purposes in us, and glorify Himself in our lives.

It is well and necessary from time to time to look at holiness from the human point of view, and to see our duty and responsibility; but it is equally essential and important that we should also dwell upon holiness, as in the passage before us, from the Divine standpoint, and keep well in view the glorious realities of God's faithfulness, God's power, God's grace. To be occupied unduly with self in the matter of holiness is to become self-centred, morbid, fearful, and weak; to be occupied with God is to be restful, quiet, strong, confident, and ever growing in grace.

III.

APPROBATION AND BLESSING.

"Wherefore also we pray always for you, that our God would count you worthy of this calling, and fulfil all the good pleasure of His goodness, and the work of faith with power: that the name of our Lord Jesus Christ may be glorified in you, and ye in Him, according to the grace of our God and the Lord Jesus Christ."—2 THESS. i. ii, 12.

Two words sum up the Christian life—Grace and Glory; and both are associated with the two Comings of the Lord Jesus Christ: Grace particularly with the first Coming, and Glory especially with the second. This twofold aspect of Christianity comes before us in the prayer of the Apostle which we now have to consider.

1. THE REASON OF THE PRAYER.

This thought is brought before us very clearly in the Revised Version: "*To which end we also pray.*" In the Authorised Version it is: "*Wherefore also we pray.*" Following the original, the R.V. refers definitely to what has preceded. The whole context is a reason for the prayer which now follows.

The *Triumphant Future* is part of the reason of his prayer. "When He shall come to be glorified in His saints, and to be marvelled at in all them that believe in that day." The Apostle looks forward to "the crowning day" that is coming, and bases upon this glorious hope the prayer that follows.

The *Testing Present* is another part of the reason for this prayer. The Church of Thessalonica was suffering persecutions and afflictions, and was passing through the fire of testing (vers. 4-7); and it was this fact—their then-existing severe experiences—that prompted the Apostle to pray for them, as well as to express the hope concerning their deliverance from the furnace of affliction.

Thus present and future are blended in his thought, and form the ground or reason of his intercession.

2. THE NATURE OF THE PRAYER.

Two elements sum up this beautiful prayer.

He asks for the *Divine Approval* on their life: "That God may count you worthy of your calling." God's "calling" is His summons into His kingdom. The kingdom may be regarded both as present and future. In the Gospels it would seem as though the "calling" were limited to His invitation or appeal, while in the Epistles it appears to include the believer's response to the call. For this reason it is sometimes spoken of as God's "calling," and at others, as in this case, as "your calling." The thought of a Divine calling responded to by the believer is prominent in the teaching of St. Paul, and should be carefully studied. Even in these Epistles to the Thessalonians, the idea is frequently found (1 Thess. ii. 12, iv. 7, v. 24; 2 Thess. ii. 14).

"Count you worthy" is a notable phrase repeated from verse 5: "Counted worthy of the kingdom of God." Seven times this verb is used by St. Paul. As we ponder it we catch something of the wondrous glory of our life as contemplated by the King of Kings. Surely, it may be said, the believer can never be "worthy"; and this is true if he is considered in himself. But just as it is with justification, which means "accounted just," so with sanctification—by the unspeakable grace of God we are actually "counted worthy." Hooker's well-known words about justification may be quoted in this connection as illustrating the thought of worthiness in sanctification. "God doth justify the believing man, yet not for the worthiness of his belief, but for His worthiness Who is believed." So we may say, God doth count the believing man worthy, yet not for any personal worthiness, but for the worthiness which is wrought by grace. We must, however, not fail to notice that the believer is responsible for his use of grace, and that the very thought of God counting us worthy has included in it the thought of scrutiny with a view to decision.

He seeks the *Divine Blessing* on their life: "And fulfil every desire of goodness and every work of faith with power." This, which is the rendering of the R.V., seems, on the whole, the more intelligible and appropriate. It means, "all that goodness can desire, and all that faith can effect." It blends together the two ideas of *aspiration* and *activity*—the aspiration of goodness and the activity of trust—and it prays that God would fulfil *with power*, or powerfully, every aspiration that comes from goodness, and every activity that springs from faith. Just as in the familiar words of the Collect for Easter Day, God first puts into "our minds good desires," and then by His "continual help" we are enabled to "bring the same to good effect." By "His holy inspiration we think those things that are good, and by His merciful guiding we perform the same."

3. THE CONSEQUENCES OF THE PRAYER.

Notice the twofold consequence here stated.

He expects that *God will be glorified in us*. Glory in the New Testament, and, indeed, in the whole Bible, is the outshining of splendour, and the Apostle seeks in answer to prayer that Christ may reveal in our lives the glory of His grace. This includes both our present and future lives. Christ is to be manifested by and glorified in us here, and He will be manifested by and glorified in us hereafter (ver. 10). What an unspeakable privilege and what a profound responsibility lie in this simple fact that Christ is to shine forth from our lives, and that men around us are to see something of Christ as they associate with us. One of the most beautiful testimonies ever given to a Christian was that of a poor dying outcast girl to a lady who had befriended her: "I have not found it hard to think about God since I knew you."

He also expects that *we shall be glorified in Christ*. This is, in a way, more wonderful still. There is to be a reciprocal glory; and, actually, marvellous though it seems, we are to have our share of glory in Christ. This, again, has its application to the present, as well as to the future, for every life that is loyal to Christ is glorified in union and communion with Him. And in the great future it will be seen and known on every hand who have been faithful to their Lord and Master. "Then shall the righteous shine forth as stars in the kingdom of their Father."

4. THE GUARANTEE OF THE PRAYER.

The Apostle scarcely ever prayed without reminding himself and his readers of the secret whereby prayer is answered. Accordingly he closes this prayer with a reminder that the guarantee of its fulfilment is the grace of God—"According to the grace of our God and the Lord Jesus Christ."

God is the *Source* of all grace. How lovingly the Apostle speaks of "our God" and "our Lord Jesus" in this verse! Elsewhere in his Epistles we also find this appropriating phrase, "Our God" (1 Thess. ii. 2, iii. 9; 1 Cor. vi. 11). As in the still more personal phrase, "My God," which we find about seven times in his writings, St. Paul expresses his consciousness of personal possession and the blessed reality of fellowship with God. "This God is *our* God," as the Psalmist says.

Christ is the *Channel* of grace. The Lord Jesus Christ being associated with God in this connection is a reminder that it is "the grace of our Lord Jesus Christ" as much as the grace of our God. He mediates grace to us, and through faith in Christ we are linked to God as the "God of all grace."

What a cheer and inspiration it is to have the assurance and guarantee that even a prayer like this, with its high standard and far-reaching possibilities, can and will be answered. Christianity provides not only an appeal, but a dynamic. He Who bids, enables; He Who calls, provides. The Gospel of Jesus Christ is at once a precept, a promise, a provision, and a power. The religions of the world often tell us to "Be good," but it is left for Christianity to proclaim that "He died *to make us good.*" As a result, the Christian can say with Augustine: "Give what Thou commandest and then command what Thou wilt." That is: "Only give me the spiritual power, and then I can do anything that Thou requirest of me." As the Psalmist cried: "I will run in the path of Thy commandments, when Thou hast set my heart at liberty."

Thus the Christian life is at once a life of Grace and a life of Glory. "First Grace, then Glory." "No Grace, no Glory." "More Grace, more Glory." "If Grace, then Glory."

> "Grace, 'tis a charming sound,
> Harmonious to the ear;
> Heaven with the echo shall resound,
> And all the earth shall hear."

IV.

LOVE AND PEACE.

"The Lord direct your hearts into the love of God, and into the patience of Christ."—2 THESS. iii. 5, R.V.

"The Lord of peace Himself give you peace always by all means."—2 THESS. iii. 16.

It is striking to note the number of prayers in these two short Epistles to Thessalonica. They are probably the earliest of the Apostle's writings, and the frequency of his prayers is a significant testimony to his thought for his converts and their needs.

Hardly less striking is the variety of the prayers, of which we have already had several proofs. There are still two prayers to be considered in the second Epistle, very terse petitions, yet full of suggestiveness and importance. It will be convenient to consider these two together, not only because of their brevity, but also because of the spiritual connection between them.

1. THE GOAL.

The context of the prayer is noteworthy. The Apostle had been asking for their prayers, more particularly for deliverance from evil men. Then comes the strong assurance that God in His faithfulness would keep them from evil, together with the expression of his own personal confidence concerning them that they would be faithful to his counsels and commands. And then follows the prayer of our text in which he asks that their hearts may be directed to that Divine goal which is, and ever must be, the true home of the soul.

"*Your hearts.*" Once again does the Apostle lay stress on this central reality of their spiritual and moral being. The heart is the citadel of the life, and the usage of the term in the Word of God must ever be kept clearly before us. It includes, as we have already seen, intellectual, emotional, and volitional elements. There is no such contrast in the New Testament between "the head" and "the heart" as we are now often accustomed to make, for intellect, feelings, and will are all comprised in the Biblical meaning. If, therefore, the heart is right, all else will be right. It was for this reason that Solomon gave the counsel to keep the heart "above all keeping," since "out of it are the issues of life."

"*Into the love of God.*" The phrase seems to suggest the direction of the heart towards a goal—"*Into* the love." This must mean first and foremost the love of God to us, for this is the true goal and home of the soul. Home is at once a protection, a fellowship, and a joy. "There's no place like home;" and there is no place like the love of God as a home for the soul. In that love we find constant protection, for all the refuge and safety of a true home are experienced there. In that love we find the fullest, truest fellowship, for "truly our fellowship is with the Father, and with His Son Jesus Christ"; and we know also "the fellowship of the Holy Ghost." Not least of all, in this home of the soul, is perfect and permanent satisfaction. Just as when the door closes upon us and we know that we are within the privacy, comfort, cheer, and fellowship of home, we find blessed restfulness and satisfaction, so when the soul enters the home of God's love it soon realises the fulness of satisfaction, for it is "satisfied with favour, full with the blessing of the Lord." Love that is deep, unfathomable, constant, pure, unchanging, Divine, is our everlasting home. It is recorded that Spurgeon once saw a weathercock with the words on it, "God is love." On remarking to the owner that it was very inappropriate, since God's love did not change like a weathercock, he received the reply that the real meaning was, "God is love whichever way the wind blows." This is the experience of the believer. Whatever comes, wherever he is, he knows that "God is love."

It is possible, perhaps probable, that this phrase, "the love of God," may also include our love to God. At any rate, in several passages it is almost impossible to make a rigid distinction between the two ideas (cf. Rom. v. 5). The one is the source of the other, and "we love Him because He first loved us." Love from God begets love to God, and when once the soul has entered into God's love as its goal and home, love at once begins to be the spring, the strength, the sustenance, and the satisfaction of its life.

"*Into the patience of Christ.*" The Authorised Version has somewhat misread this verse by translating it "into the patient waiting for Christ," which would need another expression in the Greek. It really refers to active, persistent, steady endurance rather than to patient waiting. It refers to present patience, not to a future prospect. The patience of Christ must mean the active endurance which is like His, the endurance of which He is the pattern. How marvellously He "endured the contradiction of sinners against Himself"! How striking is the statement that "He set His face steadfastly to go to Jerusalem"! Whether in suffering or in service, our Lord "endured as seeing Him who is invisible"; and having endured to the end, He became our Saviour.

But "the patience of Christ" is also the endurance which comes from Him. He is not only our pattern, but also our power, since He enables us to endure with a like endurance to His own. As the Apostle says elsewhere: "I have power for all things in Him who is empowering me." To have a pattern without the power to realise it, to have our Lord's example without His efficacy and energy, would be of little practical use except to discourage and to mock us; but He who sets the standard supplies the strength, and our hearts are thus enabled to enter into and abide in the endurance of Christ.

The need of patient endurance is obvious. Those early Christians of Thessalonica were soon put to the test. A few days and their new-born experiences were severely proved. Persecution, ostracism, suffering, and, it may be, death put a real strain upon their Christian profession; yet they endured, and the Apostle's prayer was answered; for we know with what joy he received tidings of their endurance and continuance (ch. i. 4). The same endurance is needed to-day, though the circumstances are very different. Sin is still powerful, and trials, suffering, sorrow and death are found on every hand. Many things would tempt us from our allegiance and continuance. Like the Psalmist, we see the wicked prospering, and we are ready to burst out with the faithless cry: "I have cleansed my heart in vain, and washed my hands in innocency." Or we have been toiling in the vineyard for long without seeing any fruit, and like the prophet, we are tempted to cry: "I have laboured in vain, I have spent my strength for nought." Then we hear the voice of the Apostle reminding us of "the love of God" and "the patience of Christ."

The secret of patience is love. If only we live in the love of God we shall thereby find the grace of patience. The union of love and patience was exemplified in our Lord's earthly life. He kept His Father's commandments and abode in His love, and if only we will continue in His love we shall thereby be enabled to keep His commandments, and endure as He endured.

2. THE GUIDE.

"The Lord direct your hearts." We need direction. Sin has blinded us, and kept us from knowing the way home into the love of God, and into the endurance of Christ. Still more, sin has biassed our hearts, and kept us from going along the way. Thus we need nothing short of a Divine direction. If the Lord does not make straight our way home we never shall arrive there.

How does our Lord direct our hearts? First, by constant and ever-increasing experience of His love. "God is love," and as it is of the essence of love to communicate itself, God is ever revealing to our hearts and bestowing upon them His own Divine love. Along the straight pathway He guides the soul into deeper and fuller experience of His unchanging, unerring, and unending love.

He also guides by bestowing upon us an ever-fuller experience of the power of Christ. Patient endurance is not learned all at once, and the Lord leads us as we are able to bear His disclosures and His discipline. Every lesson of testing brings with it a fresh experience of grace, and every call to endure carries with it the assurance of sufficient strength and power.

The means used for our direction, as we have already seen, are three in number, but the truth is so important that it needs renewed emphasis. The Lord directs us *by His Word*. Its examples, its counsels, its promises, its warnings, it anticipations, its incentives all come with force and blessing upon the heart, impelling it to go the right way home. He also directs us *by His Holy Spirit* dwelling within us. The Divine Spirit possesses and purifies our thoughts, cleanses and clarifies our motives, freshens and fertilises our soul, sanctifies and sensitises our conscience, guides and guards our will; and thus "every virtue we possess, and every victory won, and every thought of holiness" are the work of the Holy Spirit of God in guiding and directing our hearts into the love of God and into the patience of Christ.

The Lord also guides *by His Providence*. He uses the circumstances of our daily life to indicate His will. The discipline, the thousand and one little events and episodes, the ordinary experience of daily duty, the shadows and the sunshine, are all part of His providential guidance as He leads us along the pathway home into the love of God. All things are continually working together for good to them that love God.

Now we pass to consider the second and complementary prayer.

3. THE GIFT.

In this concluding prayer of the Epistle the Apostle sums up by speaking of that which is in some respects the greatest gift of God in Christ, the gift of perfect and perpetual peace.

Our first need is *peace of conscience*. The burden of sin weighs heavily upon the awakened soul, and the condemnation of the law consciously weighs upon it. As we look back over the past, and realise what it has been, we long for rest in the removal of condemnation and the bestowal of forgiveness. Our hearts cry out for peace with God.

Our second need is *peace of heart*. The soul set free from the burden of condemnation and guilt soon finds the need of a new strength, new interests, new hopes. The past has been obliterated by mercy, but the present looms large with difficulty. Temptations to fear and discouragement arise, and the soul longs for peace. Peace with God by reconciliation must therefore be followed by the peace of God through restfulness of heart day by day.

Our third need is *peace of fellowship*. The true Christian life is never solitary, but is lived in association with others. Our relationship to Christ necessarily carries with it a relationship to those who are in Christ with us, and as a consequence the peace which is ours in Christ is expressed in peace and fellowship with our fellow-believers. The context of this prayer shows that the Apostle had this aspect of peace in mind, and no true peace can be enjoyed with God that is not shared with our fellow-Christians. Our Lord has broken down the wall of partition between us; He has made us all one in Himself, for He is our peace.

4. THE GIVER.

The source of this threefold peace is *"The Lord of peace Himself."* By His death He brings us peace of conscience, by His Resurrection life peace of heart, by His Holy Spirit peace of fellowship. "Peace I leave with you" is the legacy of His Death. "My peace I give unto you" is the gift of His Spirit. On the Resurrection evening He came with this twofold peace. First, He said, "Peace be unto you," and "showed them His hands and His side," thus assuring them of peace of conscience through His Death. Then He said unto them *again*, "Peace be unto you," and bestowed upon them His Holy Spirit, thus guaranteeing to them peace of heart. His own peace, which had been so marked a feature of His own life and ministry, was now to be theirs. He, the possessor of peace, was now to be the provider of peace to them.

The title, "The Lord of peace," in this passage is very noteworthy. It is only found here, though the title "God of peace" occurs several times. What are we to understand by it? Surely it is a hint to us that only in His Lordship, acknowledged and experienced by us, can we find peace. In very significant words we read in the prophet of "His government and peace." First government and then peace, since peace is only possible as a result of government. In like manner we read in the psalm of "righteousness and peace," for it is only as He is "the Lord our righteousness" that He becomes the Lord our peace. When the government is upon His shoulder, and He is the Lord of our life, the inevitable and blessed result is "peace, perfect peace."

The continuity of this peace is very noteworthy—"Give you peace *always*." It is a constant peace. It is independent of circumstances, and does not change with changing experiences, since it is independent of our variableness, and depends entirely upon the Lord of peace and His Divine gift. Peace is associated with our permanent relationship to God in Christ, and a relationship of this kind is unalterable by any experiences or circumstances. The Lord gives peace always.

The channels of this peace are also significant—"Peace always *by all means.*" "In every manner," by all conceivable channels and methods this peace comes. No circumstance or condition of life can be ours which does not give some opportunity for the bestowal, experience, and enjoyment of peace. Not only does peace come "always," but "all ways."

Love, Patience, Peace—how beautiful and suggestive the combination and association! Patience is the fruit of love, and peace is the fruit of patience. When the soul is dwelling in the love of God patience and peace flow naturally into the life, and are as naturally exemplified in it. And so the heart rejoices in the love, reproduces the patience, and reposes in the peace of the Lord of peace, because it is ever at rest in the presence and grace of "the God of love and peace."

V.

KNOWLEDGE AND OBEDIENCE.

"For this cause we also, since the day we heard it, do not cease to pray for you, and to desire that ye might be filled with the knowledge of His will in all wisdom and spiritual understanding; that ye might walk worthy of the Lord unto all pleasing, being fruitful in every good work, and increasing in the knowledge of God; strengthened with all might, according to His glorious power, unto all patience and long-suffering with joyfulness; giving thanks unto the Father."—COL. i. 9-12.

The Epistles of the (first) captivity of the Apostle (Philippians, Ephesians, Colossians, Philemon) represent his maturest experiences. As a consequence the prayers found in them are particularly noteworthy, revealing some of the deepest things of the writer's spiritual life. In this respect they are at once tests and models for us; and it is perhaps not too much to say that careful and prolonged prayerful meditation on the prayers found in these Epistles will prove one of the most valuable and helpful methods of deepening the spiritual life. The first of these we now consider.

1. THE REASON OF THE PRAYER.

Colosse was one of the Churches which Paul had neither founded nor visited (ch. ii. 1). Christianity was brought there by Epaphras, one of his disciples (ch. i. 7). But the Apostle was as keenly interested in its spiritual welfare as if he had been instrumental in founding it. So when he had heard of their faith and love (ch. i. 4), and the fruitfulness of their life (ch. i. 6), he thanked God on their behalf (ch. i. 3), and prayed this prayer. Deep interest in the spiritual life of others was one of the prominent marks of the Christian character of St. Paul. His was no self-centred life, for he was ever keenly alert to appreciate the marks of grace in others. This is a test, and at the same time a rebuke, for us. How unlike we are to a Christian of the type of Barnabas, of whom we read: "Who, when he came, and had seen the grace of God, was glad" (Acts xi. 23). This is only possible by having "a heart at leisure from itself"; and when we are thus deeply interested in the marks and manifestations of the Divine working in other people's lives we shall not only praise God on their behalf, but also, like the Apostle, pray for them; and thus the blessing will extend and deepen.

2. THE NATURE OF THE PRAYER.

The main point of his prayer was that they might be *"filled with the knowledge of His will."* The will of God known and done is the secret of all true living. It was the key-note of our Lord's earthly life. He came to do the will of the Father, and in one of the deepest experiences of His life He said: "Not My will, but Thine be done." He told His disciples that His meat was to do the will of Him that sent Him; and He taught them to pray, "Thy will be done in earth as it is in heaven." The will of God is the substance of revelation, for what is the Bible from beginning to end but the revelation of God's will for man? Perhaps the most all-embracing prayer is: "Teach me to do Thy will"; and certainly the ideal life is summed up in the phrase, "He that doeth the will of God abideth for ever." Well might the Apostle pray for these Christians of Colosse to be filled with the knowledge of God's will.

The word rendered "knowledge" means "mature knowledge," and is one of the characteristic words of these four Epistles written from Rome. The Apostle evidently regarded mature knowledge, or deep spiritual experience, as the pre-eminent mark of a ripening Christian. In this respect St. John bears the same testimony, in his reference to the three stages of the Christian life represented by "little children," "young men," and "fathers." The little children *have*; the young men *are*; the fathers *know* (1 John ii. 12-14). This spiritual knowledge or experience is the great safeguard against error, in that it gives power to distinguish between good and evil, between truth and falsehood.

The measure of this knowledge is to be carefully noted—*"filled with* the knowledge of His will." The word also implies a fulness which is realised continually—not a bare knowledge, but its completeness; not an intermittent stream, but a perpetual flow. When the soul experiences this it is provided not only with the greatest safeguard against danger, but also with the secret of a strong, growing, powerful Christian life.

The characteristics of this knowledge should be observed: *"In all wisdom and spiritual understanding."* "Wisdom" is a general term which implies the capacity and faculty for adapting the best means to bring about the best ends in things spiritual. "Spiritual understanding" is the specific coming or putting together of principles by means of which true action is taken. It really means "putting two and two together," comparing ideas and principles, for the purpose of adopting the best in any given course of action. Of the importance and necessity of wisdom and spiritual understanding scarcely anything need be said. Christian wisdom, Christian understanding, Christian perception in the thousand and one things of life—this surely is one of our greatest necessities and choicest blessings.

How many errors would be avoided, how many wanderings checked, by means of this spiritual wisdom! Still more, how much joy would be experienced and how much genuine service rendered, if we were always saying and doing the right thing, at the right time, in the right way.

"Filled with the knowledge of His will in all wisdom and spiritual understanding." This means for its complete realisation constant touch with that Book which presents the clearly expressed will of God. The will of God is in that Word, and when the Word is illuminated by the Spirit of God we come to know His will concerning us. No one will ever have the full knowledge of that will, no one can possibly be mature in experience, if the Word of God is not his daily, definite, direct study and meditation. It purifies the perception of the faculties by its cleansing power; it illuminates the moral faculties with its enlightening power; it controls the emotional faculties with its protective power; it energises the volitional faculties with its stimulating power; and thus in the constant, continuous use of the Word of God in personal practice, with meditation and prayer, we shall become "filled with the full knowledge of His will in all wisdom and spiritual understanding."

3. THE PURPOSE OF THE PRAYER.

Knowledge is not an end in itself, but the means to an end; and so the Apostle states the purpose for which he asks this knowledge of God's will: *"That ye might walk worthy of the Lord unto all-pleasing ... fruitful ... increasing ... strengthened ... giving thanks."*

Their life is to be influenced by this knowledge—*"walk worthy of the Lord."* Knowledge is to be translated into practice. "Walking" is the characteristic Bible word descriptive of the character of the Christian life, the full expression of all our powers. As it presupposes life, so it means energy, movement, progress; and for this, knowledge is essential. How can we walk unless we know why and whither we go? The knowledge of God's will gives point and purpose to the activities of life.

"Walk worthy of the Lord." What a profound and searching thought is here— "Worthy of the Lord." Surely this is impossible; yet these are the plain words of the inspired writer. To walk worthy of the Lord—it is almost incredible, and yet this is one of the possibilities and glories of grace. The Apostle is fond of the word "worthy." We are to walk worthy of our vocation (Eph. iv. 1), worthy of the Gospel (Phil. i. 27), worthy of the saints (Rom. xvi. 2), worthy of God (1 Thess. ii. 12). We may be perfectly sure that Paul would not put such an ideal before us if it could not be realised. God's commands always imply promises.

"*Unto all pleasing.*" Bishop Moule beautifully renders this phrase: "Unto every anticipation of His will" (Colossian Studies). "Teach me to do the thing that pleaseth Thee" (P. B. version). What a glorious ideal! We are so to walk as to please Him in everything. Not only doing what we are told, but anticipating His commands by living in such close touch with Him that we instinctively know the thing that will please Him. These words sound a depth of the spiritual life with which comparatively few are familiar; and yet here they are, facing us definitely, with their call to realise that which God has placed before us.

The specific details of this worthy walk are next brought before us in four pregnant phrases:

"*Being fruitful in every good work.*" Notice every word of this sentence. Our life is to be characterised by good works, and in each and every one of these we are to be fruitful, manifesting the ripeness, and, if it may be so put, the beauty and lusciousness associated with fruit. Mark, too, that it is "fruitful *in* every good work," that is, in the process of doing the work, and not merely as the result or outcome of it. The very work itself is intended to be fruitful apart from particular results. There may be very few results of our service for God, but the service itself may and should be fruitful.

"*Increasing in the knowledge of God.*" Notice the difference between the knowledge of His will and the knowledge of Himself. "That I may know *Him*" (Phil. iii. 10); "They might know *Thee*" (John xvii. 3); "Ye have known *Him*" (1 John ii. 13). The knowledge of His will will lead us to the knowledge of Himself, and beyond this it is impossible to go.

"*Strengthened with all might, according to His glorious power, unto all patience and longsuffering with joyfulness.*" The Apostle's thought pours itself out in rich abundance in these words. It seems as though he could not adequately express the possibilities and characteristics of the Christian life about which he prays. They are to be "strengthened," and not only so, but "with all might." The principle or standard of it is "according to His glorious power," and the end of it is "unto all patience and longsuffering with joyfulness." The man of the world might see in this phrase an anticlimax, when it is said that the end of strength is patience and longsuffering; and yet Christianity finds its ideal in energy expressed in character, activity manifesting itself in passivity, and might in meekness.

Notice, too, the suggestive addition, "*with joyfulness.*" Patience and longsuffering without joy are apt to be cold, chilly, unattractive. There is a stern, stoical endurance of suffering which, while it may be admired sometimes, tends to repel. But when patience and longsuffering are permeated and suffused with joyfulness, the very life of Christ is lived over again in His followers. Resignation to the will of God is only very partially a

Christian virtue; but when we take joyfully the things that come upon us we are indeed manifesting the very life of God Himself.

"*Giving thanks unto the Father.*" This is the crowning grace for which the Apostle prays—thankfulness. How much it means. The heart full of gratitude and gladness, the life full of brightness and buoyancy, the character full of vitality and vigour. The joy of the Lord is, indeed, the strength of His people, and when this element of thanksgiving characterises our life, it gives tone to everything else, and crowns all other graces.

4. THE CHARACTER OF THE PRAYER.

We have seen what the Apostle desired for the Christians of Colosse, and in so doing we have learnt some of the deepest secrets of Christian living. It remains to notice the characteristics of this prayer, in order that our prayers may be taught and guided and inspired with power.

His prayer was *urgent*—"*Since the day we heard.*" From the moment the tidings came by Epaphras of the Christian life in Colosse the Apostle's heart went up to God in prayer.

His prayer was *incessant*—"*Do not cease to pray.*" Again and again he asked, and kept on asking, so fully was his heart drawn out in prayer for these Christians whom he had never seen.

His prayer was *intense*—"*And to desire.*" This was no mere lip service. His heart had evidently been stirred to its core by the tidings of the Christian life at Colosse, and as he heard of their faith, their love, their hope, their holiness, their service, a deep, intense, longing desire came into his soul to seek for still fuller and deeper blessing on their behalf. What a man he was, and what prayers his were!

His prayer was *offered in fellowship with others*—"*Since the day we heard.*" Timothy was associated with the Apostle in these petitions. United prayer is one of the greatest powers in the Christian Church. "If two of you shall agree as touching anything that they shall ask, it shall be done." Personal prayer is precious, united prayer is still more powerful.

Thus in these verses we have one of the fullest, deepest and most precious of the Apostle's prayers, and as we consider its union of thought and experience, of profound teaching and equally profound revelation of Christian life, we learn two of the most urgent and necessary lessons for the Christian life to-day.

The first of these shall be given in the words of Bishop Moule: "Beware of untheological devotion." If devotion is to be real it should be characterised by *thought*. There is no contradiction between mind and heart, between theology and devotion. Devotional hours do not mean hours when thought is absent. Meditation is not abstraction, nor is devotion dreaminess. "Thou shalt love the Lord thy God with all thy *mind*" is an essential part of the commandment. If genuine thought and equally genuine theology do not characterise our hours of devotion, we lose some of the most precious opportunities of grace and blessing. A piety which is mere pietism, an evangelicalism which does not continually ponder the profound truths of the New Testament, can never be strong or do any deep service. We must beware of "untheological devotion."

We must also beware of "undevotional theology." This is the opposite error, and constitutes an equally great danger. A hard, dry, intellectual study of theology will yield no spiritual fruit. Accuracy in knowledge of Greek, careful balancing of aspects of truth, large knowledge of the doctrinal verities of the New Testament, are all essential and valuable; but unless they are permeated by a spirit of devotion they will fail at the crucial point. *Pectus facit theologum*—it is the heart that makes the theologian; and a theology which does not spring from spiritual experience is doomed to decay, to deadness, and therefore to disaster.

When, therefore, our devotions are theological, and our theology is devotional, we begin to realise the true being, blessing, and power of the Christian life, and we go from strength to strength, from grace to grace, and from glory unto glory.

VI.

CONFLICT AND COMFORT.

"For I would that ye knew what great conflict I have for you, and for them at Laodicea, and for as many as have not seen my face in the flesh; that their hearts may be comforted, being knit together in love, and unto all riches of the full assurance of understanding, to the acknowledgment of the mystery of God, and of the Father, and of Christ."—COL. ii. 1, 2.

Although he was in prison the Apostle was constantly at work for his Master, and not least of all at the work of prayer. If ever the words *orare est laborare*, "to pray is to labour," were true, they were true of St. Paul, for to him to pray was to work with all his might, as we shall see from a study of another of the prayers offered in his Roman prison.

1. WHAT PRAYER MEANS.

Prayer is described as a *conflict*. We have a similar expression used of the prayers of Epaphras, in the words "labouring fervently" (Col. iv. 12). The same word "conflict" is associated with faith, "the good fight of faith" (1 Tim. vi. 12), and with the "good fight" of the Apostle's entire life (2 Tim. iv. 7). Prayer regarded as a conflict includes the two ideas of toil and strife.

The toil of prayer shows us the work involved in it. Sometimes we hear the expression, "If you can do nothing else, you can pray," as though prayer were the easiest of all things. As a simple fact, it is the hardest. No man knows what prayer means unless he knows what it is to "labour" in prayer. The strife involved in prayer implies opposition—the opposing force of one who wishes above all things to check and thwart our prayers. We discern something of this opposition in the well-known words, "We wrestle" (Eph. vi. 12); and the words of the hymn are as true as they are familiar—

> "And Satan trembles when he sees
> The weakest saint upon his knees."

The Apostle knew by spiritual experience that to pray was to rouse up against himself a mighty opposition, and it was this force that made his prayer such a "great conflict." No believer should be surprised at his prayers "being hindered" (1 Pet. iii. 7). It is evidently one of Satan's main objects to get the Christian to restrain prayer. The Christian man or the Christian Church that continues instant in prayer may rest assured of malignant opposition from the hosts of spiritual wickedness in high places. On the other hand, we may be sure that Satan scarcely troubles himself about the believer or congregation whose private, family, and public praying is neglected or thought little of. Prayer is, therefore, a "great conflict." It is not solicitude only, but a struggle; not merely anxiety, but activity. As Bishop Moule says: "Prayer is never meant to be *indolently* easy, however simple and reliant it may be. It is meant to be an infinitely important transaction between man and God. And therefore very often, when subjects and circumstances call for it, it has to be viewed as a work involving labour, persistency, conflict, if it would be prayer indeed" (*Colossian Studies*, p. 124). The Bishop goes on to quote a familiar incident which illustrates this great truth: "A visitor knocked betimes one morning at the door of a good man, a saint of the noblest Puritan type—and that was a fine type indeed. He called as a friend to consult a friend, sure of his welcome. But he was kept waiting long. At last a servant came to explain the delay: 'My master has been at prayer, and this morning he has been long in getting access.'"

The practical question for us is whether this is our idea of prayer, or whether we are merely playing at prayer, and not regarding it with true seriousness. If we know what it is to have "great conflict" in prayer, happy are we. If we do not, we may well ask God to search our hearts and change our minds about prayer.

Prayer is characterised by *unselfishness*. The conflict of the Apostle was not self-centred. It was on behalf of others: "Great conflict I have for you, and for them at Laodicea." This is the essence of prayer—intercession on behalf of others. If our seasons of prayer are largely taken up with prayers for our own needs, however genuine, we are failing at a crucial point; but if our time is mainly taken up with prayers for others, we shall soon find that our own blessings begin to abound. "There is that scattereth and yet increaseth."

Prayer also implies *sympathy*. The Apostle was praying for people whom he had never seen, and probably never would see. This is not easy—indeed, is very difficult—but it is a real test of spirituality. "Out of sight, out of mind." We are tempted to limit our prayers to friends whom we know, causes in which we are interested, subjects spiritually near and akin to us. Not so the Apostle, whose heart went out to the whole Church of God in every place where he knew through friends that little bodies of Christians were to be found. His sympathy was at once quick, wide, and deep, and it is one of the supreme tests of true spirituality to have a sympathy possessed of all these three characteristics. Our sympathy may be quick and yet narrow, or wide but not deep, or even deep and not wide; but to be at once quick, wide, and deep in sympathy is to be a true follower of Christ.

As we ponder these things—conflict, unselfishness, sympathy—do not our hearts condemn us? Instead of conflict, how easy-going have been our prayers! Instead of unselfish, how self-centred, instead of sympathetic, how contracted! Thus the Apostle searches and tests us as we dwell on his wonderful life of prayer.

2. WHAT PRAYER BRINGS.

What were the objects for which the Apostle prayed so earnestly on behalf of these unknown Christians? What were the precise gifts that he sought for them from God? This is no unnecessary question, for the same gifts will surely be suitable to us.

He asked for spiritual *strength*: "That their hearts might be comforted." St. Paul always went to the very centre and core of things, and so we find him constantly praying with reference to the "hearts" of these Colossian Christians. Since, as we have seen, the "heart" in Scripture is the centre of our moral and spiritual being, if the heart is right, all will be right, for "out of it are the issues of life." He prays that their "hearts" might be comforted—that is, in the full sense of the word, encouraged, exhorted, strengthened. "Comfort" includes the three elements of strength, courage, and consolation. We must be strong, brave, and cheery. This is the full meaning of the term "Comforter" as applied to the Holy Spirit. He is the One Who gives strength, courage, and consolation. This, too, is the true meaning of the familiar phrase of the English Prayer Book, "Comfortable words"—words that minister strength, fortitude, and cheer. The fact that this thought of "hearts comforted" was often in the mind and on the lips of the Apostle shows the importance he attached to it (2 Thess. ii. 17; Eph. vi. 22). With hearts made strong, courageous, and cheerful, Christians can face anything; while with hearts that remain weak, fearful, and sad the Christian life is a prey to all the temptations of the Evil One. It is exactly similar with a Church or a congregation of Christians, for one of the supreme needs in any community is comforted hearts—the centres of life made strong, courageous, and happy. Then it is that Churches live, grow, extend, and witness for Christ in the demonstration of the Holy Spirit the "Comforter."

He asked for spiritual *unity*: "Being knit together in love," or, quite literally, "having been compacted in love." He prayed that these Christians might be kept together, knit together, joined together in a spirit of love. Solitary Christians are always weak Christians, for "union is strength." If Christians are not knit together, the cause of Christ must necessarily suffer, for through the severances caused by division the enemy will keep thrusting his darts. That is why the Apostle elsewhere urges them "earnestly to strive to keep the unity of the Spirit" (Eph. iv. 3). One of the greatest powers that Satan wields to-day is due to the disunion among the people of God. It is true of the Christian home, congregation, and denomination. The wedge of discord is one of the enemy's most powerful weapons. On the other hand, where the brethren dwell together in unity, the Lord commands His blessing. In almost every Epistle the Apostle emphasises unity, and we can readily understand the reason.

This unity is only possible "in love." It is the love of God *to* us that unites us to Him, and it will be the love of God *in* us that unites us to our brethren. There is no power like love to bind Christians together. We may not see eye to eye on all aspects of truth; we may not all use the same methods of worship and service, but if we love one another God dwells in us and among us, and adds His own seal of blessing to the work done for Him. Let every Christian be fully assured that in so far as he is striving, praying, and labouring for the union of God's people in love, he will be doing one of the most powerful and blessed pieces of work for his Master, and one of the greatest possible pieces of disservice to the kingdom of Satan. Contrariwise, the Christian man or Christian Church that stands out for separateness and exclusiveness is one of the best allies of Satan, and one of the most effective workers for the kingdom of darkness.

He asked for spiritual *certitude*: "Unto all riches of the full assurance of understanding." Wealth is a favourite metaphor of St. Paul, and is used to denote the fulness and abundance of the Christian life as conceived by him. Mark how he piles phrase upon phrase—"understanding," "fulness of understanding," and then "wealth of fulness of understanding." To the Apostle, the mind was one of the essential powers and principles of the Christian life. So far from thinking according to a modern fashion that the less one uses the mind the better Christian one is, St. Paul, following his Master, ever emphasised the duty and glory of loving God "with all the mind." This wealth of the fulness of "understanding" means an abundance of conviction, both intellectual and moral, that Christianity is what it claims to be, and that the Christian life is the perfect satisfaction of all the different parts of man's nature. He prays that they may "rise to the whole wealth of the full exercise of their intelligence" (Moule). Just as we find elsewhere "the fulness of faith" (Heb. x. 22), "the fulness of hope" (Heb. vi. 11), and "much fulness" (1 Thess. i. 5), so here the Apostle desires them to enjoy to the full the intelligent grasping of assurance of Christian truth which was theirs in Christ.

In the same spirit Luke writes to Theophilus: "That thou mightest know the certainty of those things wherein thou hast been instructed." A firm conviction of the understanding is one of the greatest needs, as it is also one of the greatest blessings, of the Christian life. If a Christian cannot say, "I know," "I am persuaded," he is lacking in one of the prime essentials of a vigorous experience. Let us ponder, then, this remarkable phrase, "the whole wealth of the fulness of intelligence," and see in it one of the absolute necessities of daily experience.

But how does it come? It is the result of the foregoing "comfort" and "love." Hearts made strong mean minds fully assured. Hearts full of love mean intellects full of knowledge and conviction. Let no one say that love is blind: on the contrary, it is love that sees and knows. It was the Apostle of love who was the first with spiritual insight to say, "It is the Lord," on that memorable early morning on the Lake of Galilee. It is the Christian with a heart strong and full of love who will have the "wealth of the fulness of intelligence." The same is true of a Church, for when it is strong and united in love, there will come such an influx of conviction and certitude that the world will be impressed by the demonstration of the truth of the Christian Gospel.

He asked for spiritual *knowledge*: "To the full knowledge of the mystery of God and the Father, even Christ" (not as A.V.). Here, again, we have a favourite word of these Epistles, "full knowledge," that is, ripe, mature experience; and it means the experience of all that is summed up in the one word "Christ." In view of the dangerous errors, then rife and increasing, of a special knowledge confined only to a few, to an intellectual aristocracy, the Apostle lays stress upon the possibility of every Christian becoming acquainted in personal experience with all the knowledge of God that is stored up in Christ. He declares Christ as the Image of God (ch. i. 15), as the Head of the Church (ch. i. 18), as the One in Whom all fulness dwells (ch. i. 19), as the Redeemer from sin (ch. i. 20), as the Hope of glory (ch. i. 27), as the One in Whom are hid all the treasures of wisdom and knowledge (ch. ii. 3). There is no mistiness here, no vagueness, no hesitation, no limitation, but a full, free, open opportunity for all believers to become acquainted with Christ in His Divine fulness. This is the crowning-point of the Apostle's prayer, for in the full knowledge of Christ everything else is included. This knowledge, at once intellectual, moral, and spiritual, is the safeguard from all error, the secret of all progress, and the guarantee of all blessing.

Let this prayer, then, be our constant and careful study. We shall find in it much to rebuke the shallowness, the selfishness, the dulness, and the sluggishness of our prayers; and we shall also find in it a model of instruction, and the inspiration of all true petition and intercession. The

Christian who learns from the prayers of the Apostle will learn some of the deepest secrets of the Christian life.

VII.

WISDOM AND REVELATION.

"Wherefore I also, after I heard of your faith in the Lord Jesus, and love unto all the saints, cease not to give thanks for you, making mention of you in my prayers; that the God of our Lord Jesus Christ, the Father of glory, may give unto you the spirit of wisdom and revelation in the knowledge of Him: the eyes of your understanding being enlightened; that ye may know what is the hope of His calling, and what the riches of the glory of His inheritance in the saints, and what is the exceeding greatness of His power to us-ward who believe, according to the working of His mighty power."—EPH. i. 15-19.

If prayer for others is a barometer of our own spiritual life, we can realise what St. Paul felt was necessary for himself by his prayers for others. In Ephesians there are two petitions, and nothing fuller and deeper is found in any of the Apostle's writings. This Epistle represents the high-water mark of Christian privilege and possibility.

1. THE FOUNDATION.

We see from verse 15 that his prayer is closely and definitely based on what precedes, and this introduces us to a feature not hitherto found. Up to now the prayers at the opening have been recorded almost immediately after the personal greetings. But here a long paragraph intervenes, and the prayer is not recorded until after fourteen verses full of spiritual teaching have been given. This section deserves special attention because it is the basis of the prayer. Let us review it briefly in order to obtain the true perspective of the petition.

The key-thought is in verse 3, where the Apostle praises God for having actually blessed them "with all spiritual blessings in heavenly places in Christ." Then comes a wonderful statement of the way in which these blessings had become their own. (*a*) They had been eternally purposed in God the Father (vers. 3-6*a*); (*b*) they had been historically mediated through God the Son (vers. 6*b*-12); (*c*) they had been spiritually applied by God the Spirit (vers. 12-14). And in connection with each Person of the Sacred Trinity practically the same phrase occurs in this paragraph, showing that all the blessings were given in order that they might be used for the Divine glory: "To the praise of the glory of His grace" (ver. 6); "To the praise of His glory" (ver. 12); "To the praise of His glory" (ver. 14).

Now it is upon this wealth of provision that the Apostle bases his prayer: "On this account." God had so wonderfully blessed them in Christ by His Spirit, and this fulness of blessing was so clearly intended to be used to the praise and glory of God that he could pray, as he does here, assured that the answer would come. God's revelation of Himself is invariably and inevitably the foundation of our prayers. Because of what He has done and is doing we can be sure of grace. Because His power has provided "all things that pertain to life and godliness" we can be certain of power for daily living.

2. THE APPEAL.

The names and titles of God are particularly noteworthy and are always full of spiritual significance, shedding light on the passages in which they occur. St. Paul prays to "the God of our Lord Jesus Christ." This title as it stands is unique, though already he has referred to "the God and Father of our Lord Jesus Christ" (ver. 3), and will refer again to "the Father of our Lord Jesus Christ" in connection with prayer (ch. iii. 14). "The God of our Lord Jesus Christ" seems to suggest the highest point and peak of power and grace. God, as the God of Christ, is the primary source of all blessing.

He is also "the Father of Glory." This, too, is a phrase not found elsewhere. He is the Father to Whom all glory belongs as its Divine source. In Acts vii. 2 He is "the God of glory," and in 1 Cor. ii. 8 Christ is "the Lord of glory." In Rom. vi. 4 Christ is said to have been raised from the dead "by the glory of the Father." Glory is a characteristic quality of God. It is the manifestation of His splendour and the outshining of His excellence. All radiance, all brightness, all magnificence come from Him and are intended to be returned to Him in praise. The glory of God in Romans is threefold: it is God's proof for man's past life (ch. iii. 23); it is God's prospect for man's future life (ch. v. 2); it is God's principle for man's present life (ch. xv. 7). And the association of glory with prayer seems to suggest that the praise of His glory which is to characterise our life can only come from God Himself as the Father of glory. If our lives are to be lived "to His praise," His must be the power. If our lives are to manifest His glory, His must be the grace. "Thine is the kingdom, the power, and the glory."

3. THE REQUEST.

Now we come to this profound prayer which teaches the inmost secrets of the spiritual life.

(1) A Divine Gift. "May give to you a spirit of wisdom and revelation." He has spoken of the wealth of blessing stored up in Christ (ver. 3), and of God's grace abounding to us in all wisdom and prudence (ver. 8). Now he asks for wisdom and illumination to perceive all this for themselves as a personal experience. The word "spirit" seems to refer to their human faculty, though of course as indwelt and possessed by the Divine Spirit. But the absence of the definite article from the word "spirit" seems to suggest a gift rather than a Person. The Holy Spirit of God enters into our spirit, and the result is wisdom and revelation. These two words refer to general illumination and specific enlightenment. He desires his readers to enter fully into the meaning of these great realities to which he has given such full expression (vers. 1-14).

(2) But this Divine gift is only possible by means of a simple yet important condition. It is "in the full knowledge of Him." The word rendered "knowledge" is characteristic of these prison epistles, and always means "full knowledge," the mature experience of the spiritual man. It is invariably connected with God; it refers to the deep, growing, ripening consciousness which comes from personal fellowship with Him. Philosophy can only say "Know thyself," but Scripture says, "Know God." This is how wisdom and revelation become ours, and Christian history and experience testify abundantly to the simple yet remarkable fact of spiritual insight and moral understanding which are due solely to fellowship with God. Nothing is more striking than the fact of a deep, spiritual apprehension and appreciation which are independent of intellectual conception and verbal expression. Believers can have a true spiritual consciousness of God without the possession of great capacity or attainments. Many whose natural education and intellectual opportunities have been slight have had this spiritual perception in an uncommon degree, and it always marks the spiritually ripe Christian. It is not the one whose intellectual knowledge is critical, scholarly, and profound, but he whose spiritual insight is suffused with grace, love, and fellowship. This does not mean that natural knowledge or culture is to be despised or avoided as evil, but that the two kinds of knowledge should be carefully distinguished. The Christian Church has at least for the last three hundred years set great store by knowledge and science, but deeper than all this is the spiritual instinct, insight, knowledge, and illumination which constitute the supreme requirement of the true Christian life. We can see this spiritual perception in its various stages in several passages of the New Testament. We have seen how St. John divides believers into three classes (1 John ii. 12-14). But while in his repetition the Apostle can vary the description of the "children" and the "young men," when he has to speak the second time of the "fathers" he has nothing new to say, for they cannot be otherwise or

more fully described than as those who "know Him Who is from the beginning."

(3) The immediate consequence of this fellowship is that the eyes of the heart become permanently enlightened (Greek). Keeping in view the Scripture truth of the "heart" as including the elements of Mind, Emotion, and Will, the result of fellowship with God is that every feature of the inner life becomes purified and enlightened. The mind is illuminated to perceive truth, the emotions are purified to love the good, and the will is equipped to obey the right. It is not that new objects meet the gaze so much as that a new and deeper perception is given to enable the heart to see and understand what had hitherto been dark and difficult. This illuminated heart is one of the choicest blessings of the spiritual life and one of the greatest safeguards against spiritual error. "Ye have an unction ... and ye know" (1 John ii. 20). "The Son of God hath come, and hath given us an understanding" (1 John v. 20). Many of the problems affecting the spiritual life are solved only in this way. Criticism, scholarship, intellectual power may be brought to bear upon them, but they will not yield to this treatment. The illuminated heart of the babe in Christ is often enabled to understand secrets which are hid from the wise and prudent.

(4) The outcome is a permanent spiritual experience. "That ye may know," *i.e.* possess an immediate, instinctive, direct knowledge (εἰδέναι). Three great realities are thereupon mentioned as the objects and substance of our spiritual knowledge.

(*a*) The first is "What is the hope of His calling." "His calling" is the appeal and offer of the Gospel with all its Divine meaning and purpose, and "the hope of His calling" is that which is intended by and included in the offer of God. This "hope" is either that *to* which God calls us, or *by* which He calls; either objective or subjective; either the substance or the feeling. Hope when regarded as objective, as the substance of our experience, is full of promise, on which the believer fixes his faith. Hope when regarded as subjective, as the possession of the soul, is full of inspiration, as it encourages and confirms belief that "He is faithful that promised." Hope as an objective reality is fixed on Christ, and since God has a purpose in calling us, we can exercise hope. Hope as a subjective realisation is based on the fact of experience. God calls us by the Gospel, and therefore hope becomes possible. Hope is the top-stone of life and follows faith and love (cf. ver. 15). Faith draws the curtain aside; hope gazes into the future; while love rejoices in the present possession of Christ. Faith accepts; hope expects. Faith appropriates; hope anticipates. Faith is concerned with the person who promises; hope with the thing that the person promises. Faith is concerned with the past and present; hope with the future alone. Hope is invariably fixed on the future and is never to be regarded as merely a matter of natural temperament. It is specifically connected with the Lord's Coming, and we are thus reminded that the calling of God covers past, present, and future. It starts from regeneration and culminates in the resurrection of the body at the Coming of Christ.

(*b*) The second is "The riches of the glory of His inheritance in the saints." This may mean the wealth which God possesses *for* them or *in* them; our wealth in Him or His in us. If we take it in the former sense it will mean that God is the inheritance and we are the heirs; that the saints now possess imperfectly, and anticipate in its fulness, the inheritance of grace, the spiritual Canaan which they are to enjoy here and hereafter. If, however, we take it, as is more likely, in the latter sense, it will mean that we are the inheritance and God is the Possessor and Heir. We must never forget that the Biblical ideas associated with "heir" and "inheritance" always refer to possession, and not, as in ordinary phraseology, to succession. In the Bible the heir does not merely expect, but already enjoys in part that which he will possess in full hereafter. Adopting, then, the second of these interpretations, the saints belong to God and are precious in His sight. They are His *peculium*, or special treasure, like Israel of old (Deut. iv. 20). They have been formed for Him and are to show forth His praise (Isa. xliii. 21). He sets store by them, as is suggested by the significant words, "Hast thou considered My servant Job?" There are several indications in Scripture that God values and trusts His people; "I know him, that he will command his children and his household after him" (Gen. xviii. 19). "The Lord taketh pleasure in His people" (Ps. cxlix. 4). "The steps of a good man are ordered by the Lord: and He (that is, God) delighteth in his way" (Ps. xxxvii. 23). And the "wealth" is a further proof of the value placed on believers by God. Five times in Ephesians the Apostle uses this metaphor of "riches," showing his thought of those who have been "bought with a price" (1 Cor. v. 20). Believers are God's riches, wealth, treasure; they belong to Him in view of that day on which He will enter in full upon His inheritance when He comes to be glorified and admired in them that believe (2 Thess. i. 10). And we are to see this, to know it, to realise the spiritual possibilities of each believer and all God's people together as God's own inheritance.

(*c*) The third is "the exceeding greatness of His power to us-ward who believe." In this marvellous association of almost inexpressible thoughts the dominant note is "power" (δύναμις), and the Apostle prays that the Ephesian Christians may know what this means. Power is a characteristic word of St. Paul as expressive of Christianity. The Gospel is "the power of God unto salvation" (Rom. i. 16). By the Resurrection Christ was designated "the Son of God with power" (Rom. i. 4). He is "the power of God" (1 Cor. i. 18). Man needs power, not merely a philosophy or an ethic, but a dynamic, and it is the peculiar privilege of His Gospel to bring this to us. But let us try to analyse this power. There are no less than four comparisons stated or illustrations given. (1) It is exactly the same power that God wrought in Christ at the Resurrection. Nothing less than this is the standard of the Divine working. We are to possess and experience the spiritual and moral dynamic exercised by God on Christ when He raised Him from the dead. This is described as "the exceeding greatness of His power." The same adjective is used of grace (ch. ii. 7), and of love (ch. iii. 19), and it is intended to express the superabundance of that power which was put forth in the Resurrection and is now exercised on our behalf. Then the four words used for power are particularly noteworthy: "power," "energy," "strength," "might." Each conveys an aspect of this great spiritual force. "Might" is power in *possession*; "strength" is power as the result of *grasping*, or of coming into contact with the source of that power; and "energy" is a power in *expression*. (2) Not only so, but the power exercised by God in the Ascension is also intended to be bestowed on and experienced by us. When we are told that Christ was set at God's right hand far above all powers, we can understand something of the Divine might exercised. (3) Still more, it is the same power by means of which God put all things under the feet of Christ. This, too, is the Divine force and energy for believers. (4) Not least of all, it was Divine power that gave Christ to be "the Head over all things to the Church," and it is exactly this power that is exercised on our behalf. When we contemplate all this as intended by God for us, we can see something of the vigorous and victorious life He can and will enable us to live.

As we review this wonderful prayer it is impossible to avoid noticing that the first petition refers mainly to the past ("His calling"); the second mainly to the future ("His inheritance"); and the third mainly to the present ("His power"), though of course each petition has its bearing on the other two points of time. Every part of our life is thus adequately supplied and intended to be abundantly satisfied. Nor may we omit to observe that all through the prayer the emphasis is on God: *His* calling; *His* inheritance; *His* power. Everything is regarded from the Divine standpoint, because we are not our own but His. The contemplation of this glory of the Divine love and grace overwhelms the soul with "wonder, love, and praise."

In the presence of such a prayer, dealing with such profound realities, three thoughts naturally arise in our minds. (*a*) How little we know, and how much we might and should know. (*b*) How little we are, and how much we might and should be. (*c*) How little we do, and how much we might and should do. And yet if we will but remind ourselves of the simple secret of true living, as here described, we might become and accomplish infinitely more than we have ever experienced up to the present. "To us-ward who believe." Faith is the simple yet all-sufficient secret. Trust relies on God and receives from Him. It puts us in contact with the source of blessing, and in union with Him we shall find spiritual illumination, spiritual insight, spiritual experience, and spiritual power that shall all be lived and exercised to His praise and glory.

VIII.

STRENGTH AND INDWELLING.

"For this cause I bow my knees unto the Father of our Lord Jesus Christ, of Whom the whole family in heaven and earth is named, that He would grant you, according to the riches of His glory, to be strengthened with might by His Spirit in the inner man; that Christ may dwell in your hearts by faith; that ye, being rooted and grounded in love, may be able to comprehend with all saints what is the breadth, and length, and depth, and height; and to know the love of Christ, which passeth knowledge, that ye might be filled with all the fulness of God."—EPH. iii. 14-19.

"In no part of Paul's letters does he rise to a higher level than in his prayers, and none of his prayers are fuller of fervour than this wonderful series of petitions. They open out one into the other like some majestic suite of apartments in a great palace-temple, each leading into a loftier and more spacious hall, each drawing nearer the presence chamber, until at last we stand there" (MACLAREN).

The second prayer in Ephesians possesses remarkable affinities with the first; indeed, the two are complementary, and many of the expressions call for close comparison.

1. THE STANDPOINT.

"For this cause" (ver. 14). To what does this phrase point back? Some associate it with verse 1, "For this cause," thinking that St. Paul, having been diverted from his main teaching in verses 1-13, here resumes it in the form of a prayer. But perhaps it is still better to regard the resumption of the main teaching as coming in ch. iv. 1, where the Apostle again speaks of himself as "the prisoner." This would make ch. iii. wholly parenthetical, so that instead of the present prayer being based on the teaching of ch. ii. the Apostle is led here to speak of his ministry (ch. iii. 1-13) and its outcome. His ministry is a gift, a trust, a stewardship, and its purpose is the proclamation of the Gospel and its results in the accomplishment of God's purposes for Jew and Gentile. On this view the standpoint of the prayer is associated closely with his ministry and its effects, as seen in the immediately preceding verses. It is because of his remarkable ministry, given to him by God, and all the spiritual privileges brought to the Gentile Christians thereby that he is able to work for them (ver. 13), and also to pray for them (ver. 14). Thus, while the prayer in ch. i. looks at their life from the standpoint of the Divine purposes, this prayer will be occupied with their spiritual privileges in Christ.

2. THE ATTITUDE.

"I bow my knees unto the Father" (ver. 14). The intense reverence of the Apostle in this allusion to bowing his knees is particularly noteworthy. As a rule the Jews stood for prayer (Luke xviii. 11-13), and prostration seems to have been an exceptional posture. But in connection with Christians, kneeling is mentioned (Acts vii. 60, ix. 40, xx. 36). Nothing could more beautifully express the true attitude of the soul before God than this posture of the body. At the same time the use of the word "Father" indicates the other side of the truth and confidence with which we approach God. He is at once our God and our Father (ch. i. 17), and our attitude must be expressive both of our adoration and of our assurance. He is great and good, and we approach Him as the Holy One and the Loving One.

3. THE ADDRESS.

"The Father from Whom every family in heaven and earth is named." It is interesting that the title "God" is not associated with this prayer as in ch. i., although the thought of Deity is found in the allusion to bowing the knees. And in addition to God as the Father He is described as the One "from Whom every family (Greek, 'fatherhood') in heaven and earth is named." This seems to mean that whatever element of family life exists, it comes from God, that all true spiritual life in heaven or earth has its origin in the Father. The scope of the prayer is particularly noteworthy, as we contemplate God as the Fount of every fatherhood and the Parent of all men everywhere. Such a statement will do more than anything else to guard us against narrow or purely selfish desires as we approach God in prayer.

4. THE APPEAL.

"That He would grant you" (ver. 16). As in the former prayer, the Apostle is clear that what he is about to ask is essentially a Divine gift. It comes from above, whether he is seeking knowledge (ch. i. 17) or power (ch. iii. 16). At every step God must give and the believer must receive. It would be well for us in our Christian experience to emphasise this simple but searching truth. "Every good and every perfect gift comes from above."

5. The Standard.

"According to the riches of His glory" (ver. 16). Here again we begin to realise something of the fulness of the prayer to be offered. The measure of the Apostle's desire is not our own poverty, but God's wealth; we are to look away from ourselves to the infinite riches of the Divine glory. In the former prayer he asked that we might know the riches of God's glory. But here there is something more; we are to experience them in our heart and life.

6. The Petitions.

In general St. Paul asks for two great spiritual blessings, the inward strength of the Holy Spirit and the indwelling presence of Christ. These are inseparable, and we may regard the first as essential to the second, and the second as the effect of the first. But the prayer goes into detail and each part of the petition calls for careful meditation.

(1) "Strengthened with power through His Spirit in the inward man" (ver. 16, R.V.). As wisdom was the burden of the former prayer (ch. i. 17), so strength is the main thought here. The order, too, is significant; wisdom and power, since power without knowledge would be highly dangerous. This strength comes from the Holy Spirit; He is the Agent of God's enabling grace. And the strength is to extend "into the inward man." The contrast seems to be between the inward and the outward, as in 2 Cor. iv. 16; Rom. vii. 22. The strength is not of the body, or of the mind, but of the soul. The "inward" is not exactly identical with the "new" man, but emphasises the inner essential life of the spirit as contrasted with the outer life of the body. "The hidden man of the heart."

(2) "That Christ may dwell in your hearts through faith" (ver. 17, R.V.). This is the outcome of the inward strength of the Spirit, and almost every word needs attention. The indwelling of Christ is virtually identical with that of the Spirit (ch. ii. 22), although of course Christ and the Holy Spirit are never absolutely identified in Holy Scripture (2 Cor. iii. 17, 18). It is only in regard to the practical outcome in the believer's experience that the indwelling of Christ and the Spirit amount to the same thing. This is to be a permanent indwelling and not a mere passing stay, just as believers together are described as a temple for God's permanent habitation (ch. ii. 22, Greek). This permanent indwelling of Christ is to be "in your hearts." Almost every prayer is thus concerned with the "heart," the centre of the moral being, and the Apostle prays that Christ may make His home therein. This is no mere influence, but a Personal Presence, the Living Christ within, and it is to be "through faith." It is faith that admits Christ to the

heart, allowing Him to enter into every part of the "inward man." And the same faith that admits Him permits Him to remain, reside, and rule. Faith, in a word, is the total response of the soul to the Lordship of Christ.

(3) "That ye, being rooted and grounded in love" (ver. 17). Here again the original expressions imply permanent results, and the two words "rooted" and "grounded" are beautifully complementary. The one refers to a tree, the other to a house, and the expressions point to those hidden processes of the soul which are the result of Christ's indwelling and the Holy Spirit's working. The power of the Spirit and the indwelling of Christ tend to our permanent inward establishment in the element and atmosphere of Christian love. This is one of the seven occasions in this short Epistle where we find the Pauline phrase, "in love," referring to the sphere and atmosphere of our fellowship with God. The love no doubt means primarily and perhaps almost exclusively God's love to us, as that in which we are to "live, and move, and have our being."

(4) "May be strong to apprehend with all the saints what is the breadth and length and height and depth" (ver. 18, R.V.). Here again the emphasis is on strength, and the Apostle prays that we may have full strength to grasp, may be quite able to accomplish this purpose. Spiritual ideas can never be appropriated by intellectual action alone. It is not by brilliant intellect but by spiritual insight that we become "able to comprehend." Although there is now no specific reference to love, it would seem as though the idea of verse 19 is already in view, and, assuming this to be the case, we have four aspects of the Divine love which we are to be strong to grasp. Its "breadth" means that there is no barrier to it, reminding us of the extent of the Divine counsels; its "length" tells us of the Divine foreknowledge and His thought of us through the ages; its "height" points to our Lord in heaven as the goal for the penitent believer; its "depth" declares the possibility of love descending to the lost abyss of human misery for the purpose of redemption. And the ability to grasp the Divine love in this fourfold way is to be experienced with "all the saints." It is impossible to accomplish it alone; no spiritual exclusiveness is thinkable in this connection, to say nothing of the lower forms of egotism and selfishness. Twice in this brief writing does the Apostle refer to "all the saints" (ch. vi. 18), thereby reminding us of the place and power of each saint in the spiritual economy of God. One saint will be able to comprehend a little, another saint a little more, and so on, until at length all the saints together are "strong to grasp" the Divine love. The wider our fellowship the fuller and firmer our hold of the love of Christ. This is doubtless why public worship is so strongly emphasised in the New Testament. "Where two or three are gathered together in My Name, there am I." The experiences of our fellow-worshippers are always intended to be, and usually will be, of help to our

own fuller realisation of our Lord and Master. The soul is justified solitarily and alone, but it is sanctified only in the community of believers.

(5) "And to know the love of Christ which passeth knowledge" (ver. 19). If we are correct in interpreting verse 18 of the Divine love, the present verse will be the climax of this part of the prayer, and it has been helpfully suggested that we have here the "fifth dimension" of the love of Christ after the four already mentioned. Not only are they to experience breadth and length and height and depth but also the inwardness; they are to know by personal experience the love of Christ as it can only be known by those who have fellowship with Him. It is a love that surpasses knowledge, just as His power surpasses everything (ch. i. 19). The paradox of knowing that which surpasses knowledge will not be misunderstood from the standpoint of spiritual experience, because it is the difference between apprehending and comprehending. We know, and know deeply, increasingly, blessedly, and yet all the while there are infinite stretches of love beyond our highest experiences.

(6) "That ye may be filled unto all the fulness of God" (ver. 19, R.V.). This is the climax of the prayer and is the culminating purpose of the work of the Spirit and the indwelling of Christ. Strength, indwelling, love, and knowledge are to issue in fulness, and we are to be "filled unto all the fulness of God." In the former prayer this fulness is associated with Christ and with His body the Church (ch. i. 23), but here it is specifically associated with God and ourselves as believers in Christ. When these two passages are associated with ch. v. 18, which speaks of the fulness of the Spirit, we have the word "fulness" connected with each Person of the Blessed Trinity. What it means for the soul to be filled to overflowing with the presence of God itself is beyond our comprehension; it can only be a matter of personal experience as we seek to fulfil the proper conditions. Such a prayer for the fulness of God is best expressed in Miss Havergal's words—

> "Lord, we ask it, scarcely knowing
> What this wondrous gift may be;
> But fulfil to overflowing,
> *Thy* great meaning let us see."

IX.

LOVE AND DISCERNMENT.

"And this I pray, that your love may abound yet more and more in knowledge and all judgment: that ye may approve things that are excellent; that ye may be sincere and without offence till the day of Christ; being filled with the fruits of righteousness, which are by Jesus Christ, unto the glory and praise of God."—PHIL. i. 9-11.

One of the most beautiful elements in the Pauline Epistles is the intimate relation which evidently existed between the Apostle and his converts. This is especially the case in the Epistle to the Philippians, for in no other writing is there such a full revelation of the heart of St. Paul and of his love to those with whom he was united in Christ. As, therefore, he knew them so intimately, so he prayed for them, the prayer revealing at once their need, and his conviction as to essential things. Prayer is always strong in proportion to our acquaintance with the spiritual life of others, and feeble so far as we are ignorant of their needs.

1. THE DEFINITE REQUEST.

Let us mark the opening words: "this I keep on asking" (Greek). There was one thing for which he asked continually, and this seemed to him to sum up everything in their life.

(1) He prayed for love; "your love." As they already possessed life, he wished it to be expressed in love. The Epistle is full of this subject. No writing is so truly characterised by the love of St. Paul for his converts, or of his converts for St. Paul (see ch. iv. 14-18). Let us again remind ourselves that love in the New Testament is something definite, tangible, strong, practical, intense. It is more than sentiment, though of course it includes that; it is more than emotion, though undoubtedly it includes that; it is more than desire, though obviously it includes that. Love is the outgoing of the entire nature in self-sacrificing service. It is the sympathy of the heart and the devotion of the life to its object. As such it is the supreme proof of the reality of our Christian profession. "If ye love Me, ye will keep My commandments" (John xiv. 15, R.V.). "Lovest thou Me ... feed My sheep" (John xxi. 16). "Seeing ye have purified your souls ... love one another from the heart unfeignedly" (1 Pet. i. 22, R.V.). It was with no cynicism, but with a wonderful astonishment, that the heathen used to say, "See how these Christians love one another." When therefore the Apostle prayed for love

he was asking that the Philippian Christians might possess and manifest the very finest, truest, most powerful, and most attractive proof of their Christian life.

(2) He prayed for abounding love; "that your love may abound." Not only some, but abundant love; not a little, but much. Love to be real must be kept full, intense, overflowing; it calls for continual reinforcement, replenishing, and the abundance of love is the measure and proof of the possession of abundant life.

(3) He prayed for increasing love; "that your love may abound yet more and more." Expression is piled upon expression in order to emphasise the importance of love and its progress. Love is intended to grow and not to remain stationary. Just as life makes progress, so must its result similarly develop in love. The motto for the Christian is "more and more." This is why there is so much in the New Testament about growth, for just as it is with natural life so it must be with spiritual. Constant increase, development, progress, extension, expansion must mark it at every step.

(4) He prayed for discerning love; "that your love may abound yet more and more in knowledge and all discernment" (R.V.). The two words "knowledge" and "discernment" are particularly noteworthy. One expresses the principle, the other the application. Again we observe this word "knowledge" as a characteristic expression of the Apostle in these prison-epistles. "Full knowledge" (Greek) is one of the marks of a growing Christian life, and is proved by spiritual perception, spiritual feeling, spiritual discernment. There is a world of difference between intellectual ability and spiritual insight. Many people are clever, but not spiritual, while many people are often truly spiritual without being possessed of much intellectual capacity. Much is said in Scripture about *sight* in regard to things spiritual. "Except a man be born again, he cannot *see*" (John iii. 3). "Blessed are the pure in heart, for they shall *see* God" (Matt. v. 8). There are many people in our congregations of average intellect, and perhaps with mental powers decidedly below the average, who are nevertheless full of profound spiritual wisdom because love to Christ has given them keenness of vision and depth of insight.

2. THE IMMEDIATE PURPOSE.

This constant progress and abundance of love was intended for a very practical purpose; "so that ye may approve the things that are excellent" (ver. 10, R.V.). The discernment already mentioned was intended for spiritual discrimination. They were to be enabled to distinguish, to prove, and thereby to approve. As Lightfoot points out, "love imparts a sensitiveness of touch, a keen edge to the discriminating faculty in things moral and spiritual." In things spiritual at least love is not blind, but keen-sighted. It is endowed with a spiritual discernment which is able to distinguish not only between good and bad, but between good and better, between better and best, and between best and excellent. The words, "approve the things that are excellent," occur also in Rom. ii. 18, and the meaning seems to be first that they were to "distinguish the things that differ," and then as a result they were to "approve the things that transcend." This spiritual discernment is particularly needful to-day, as the Christian soul is surrounded by so many views and voices. Much that appears on the surface to be attractive and charming contains within it the elements of spiritual danger and disaster, and it is only by spiritual discernment which comes from abounding and increasing love to Christ that the soul is safeguarded against evil and led to approve and follow the things that are superior. It is a vivid picture that the prophet gives of the Messiah when he describes Him as endowed by the Spirit of God and made of "quick scent in the fear of the Lord" (Isa. xi. 3, Hebrew). It is this "quick scent" that by the same Spirit the Lord Jesus Christ bestows upon those who love Him with all the heart.

3. THE PERMANENT RESULT.

Every Christian grace is intended for practical and permanent effect in character. Our lives are not to be intermittent, but continuous in their expression of grace and blessing, and all that the Apostle has been praying for and desiring on behalf of his Philippian Christians was intended to develop and express in them the solid and permanent realities of Christian character.

(1) Sincerity; "that ye may be sincere" (ver. 10). This has to do with motives. The word is thought to mean "tested in the sunlight." Our lives are to be manifestly true, genuine, sincere, "transparent." "Motive makes the man," and from time to time it is essential that we should allow ourselves to be tested and judged in the sunlight of our perfect fellowship with Christ, just as St. Peter, when asked by his Master, said, "Lord, Thou knowest all things." Sincerity is one of the essential features of the true Christian life. The believer, if he is to do the will of God and commend the Gospel to others, must have no doubtful *arrière pensée* but a life lived moment by moment in the perfect brightness of the presence of perfect holiness.

(2) Consistency; "void of offence" (ver. 10, R.V.). This has to do with conduct. Not only are we to be inwardly true, but outwardly sure. Our lives must not hinder others, or put a stumbling-block in their way. Just as the

Master said, "Blessed is he whosoever is not put to stumble by Me," so must it be with every follower of Christ. Our lives are to be stepping-stones, not stumbling-blocks.

(3) Character; "being filled with the fruits of righteousness." This has to do with our permanent life both within and without, though the emphasis is on being rather than on doing. Character is the highest point and peak of the Christian life, for just as fruit is the outcome of the life of a tree, so character is the fruit of Christian living, and is the best proof of its existence. The Apostle's word suggests that we are to be "permanently filled" (Greek) with the fruits of righteousness, those things that are right, straight, true, correct, upright, without any deflection on either side. The Lord Who is our Righteousness works in us the fruits of righteousness by the indwelling of the Holy Spirit.

4. THE ULTIMATE OBJECT.

The Apostle looks forward "unto the day of Christ" (ver. 10, R.V.), and then speaks of the Christian life being lived "unto the glory and praise of God" (ver. 11). Everything is to tend towards the manifestation of the splendour of God in human life whereby others will be led to acknowledge and praise Him (Matt. v. 16). And this will reach its culminating point in the "day of Christ," that time when Christian people will stand before their Master and receive the reward of their life and service rendered to Him (ch. i. 6, ii. 16). This was the Apostle's constant thought, and towards this he strained every nerve (ch. iii. 11-21). It expresses the highest ideal of Christian living, for day by day we are to live with this wonderful thought of "the glory and praise of God," and day by day we are to look forward to the coming of Christ as that day in which our life will find its fullest realisation, its complete satisfaction, and its unending joy. And all this reminds us of the essential simplicity of life, for there is nothing complex, or involved, or mysterious, or difficult in a life lived day by day to the praise of God and in the light of the coming of our Master.

As we review this prayer we may feel perfectly sure that the Apostle meant it to be answered, and indeed, he himself gives us the hint of how this may come to pass when he tells us that the fruits of righteousness are "through Jesus Christ." This is only another way of expressing what he has already shown, his confidence that the possession of the Christian life is the guarantee of its complete realisation and full perfection by the indwelling presence and work of the Lord Jesus Christ Himself (ch. i. 6). Let us therefore take heart of grace as we contemplate this prayer and the other prayers of the Apostle. We must not be depressed, or disheartened, or discouraged, as we ponder the marvellous details and contemplate the stupendous heights of the Christian life as depicted by St. Paul's wonderful spiritual insight. On the contrary, we must remind ourselves that he would not have prayed these prayers unless he had been certain that God would answer them, and they will assuredly be answered as we set ourselves resolutely, humbly, lovingly, trustfully to fulfil the required conditions, "through Jesus Christ our Lord."

APPENDIX.

Considerations of space have prevented the inclusion of all the Prayers of St. Paul, but for the treatment of the prayer in Rom. XV. 13 reference may perhaps be permitted to the author's *Royal and Loyal* (ch. v.) and to his Devotional Commentary on *Romans* (vol. iii. p. 103 ff.). And a fuller treatment of 2 Thess. iii. 16 is given in his *The Power of Peace*.

For the thorough exegetical foundation of the passages included in these prayers of the Apostle special attention should of course be given to the various modern standard Commentaries. The following have proved of particular value in the preparation of these pages. On Thessalonians: Milligan, Frame, Eadie, and Ellicott. On Romans: Sanday and Headlam, Godet, and the Notes by Lightfoot. On Ephesians: Armitage Robinson, Westcott, and Eadie. On Philippians: Lightfoot and Ellicott. On Colossians: Lightfoot and Ellicott. Preachers will find it nothing short of an education in Greek to ponder the passages under the guidance of these master-minds. The first step in all true expository preaching is the consideration of the words and phrases in order to elicit their full exegetical value. Following this, and based upon it, will come the spiritual teaching and personal application, and for this purpose the following books will be found of great value. On Thessalonians: Denney in the *Expositor's Bible*. On Romans: Bishop Moule in the same series. On Ephesians: G. G. Findlay in the *Expositor's Bible*, with R. W. Dale's well-known Lectures. On Philippians: Rainy in the *Expositor's Bible*, and Jowett's *The High Calling*. On Colossians: Maclaren's peerless treatment in the *Expositor's Bible*, with Bishop Moule's *Colossian Studies*, and a useful American work, *Oneness with Christ*, by Bishop Nicholson. The subject of this book is definitely treated in *The Prayers of St. Paul*, by W. B. Pope, D.D.; *The Pattern Prayer Book*, by E. W. Moore; *Preces Paulinæ*, a valuable old book by an anonymous author, which is now only obtainable second-hand.

On the general subject of Prayer, which will naturally be given attention in the expository preaching and teaching on this special topic of St. Paul's petitions, the following among other books may perhaps be mentioned: *Waiting on God*, by Andrew Murray; *The Hidden Life of Prayer*, by D. M. M'Intyre; *Prayer*, by M'Conkey; *Praying in the Holy Ghost*, by G. H. C. Macgregor; *Quiet Talks on Prayer*, by S. D. Gordon; and *Prayer: Its Nature and Scope*, by H. C. Trumbull.

Milton Keynes UK
Ingram Content Group UK Ltd.
UKHW050243220624
444555UK00005BA/491

9 789361 474507